Eid Stories

Eid Stories

SCHOLASTIC
New York Toronto London Auckland
Sydney New Delhi Hong Kong

This anthology © 2010 Scholastic India Pvt. Ltd.
Copyright for the individual stories rests with the authors

All rights reserved.

Published by Scholastic India Pvt. Ltd.
A subsidiary of Scholastic Inc., New York, 10012 (USA).
Publishers since 1920, with international operations in Canada, Australia, New Zealand, the United Kingdom, India and Hong Kong.

No part of this publication may be reproduced in whole or in part, or stored in a retrieval system, or transmitted in any form or by any means, electronic, mechanical, photocopying, recording, or otherwise without the written permission of the publisher.

For information regarding permission, write to:
Scholastic India Pvt. Ltd.
A-27, Ground Floor, Sigma Centre
Infocity-1, Sector 34, Gurgaon-122001 (India)

Typeset in 13/16 Venetian301 BT by SÜRYA, New Delhi

First edition: April 2010
This edition: October 2022

ISBN-13: 978-81-8477-626-3

Printed at Shivam Offset Press, New Delhi

Contents

After that, in Mumbai 1
 Paro Anand

Afifa 12
 Siddhartha Sarma

The Goat Who Got Away 23
 Samina Mishra

Badi Ammi 35
 Lovleen Misra

Azeeza's First Fast 51
 Rukhsana Khan

Sweets for Shankar 61
 Adithi Rao

Precious Gift 79
 Shahrukh Husain

Red, 17: An Eid Story 96
 Devashish Makhija

After that, in Mumbai

Paro Anand

Ayub came home from school in tears. Although his mother asked and asked and even tried to bribe him with his favorite gajar ka halwa, he was unwilling to tell her what had happened. Or maybe, he was unable to. It worried Ammi, she just didn't know what to do.

Eventually, Ayub calmed down and sat moodily munching his halwa. She decided not to drive him further into silence with her questions. That afternoon, she let him watch cartoons before his homework. Something that happened very rarely. But she was relieved when he smiled and her heart sang out when she heard him giggle at the screen.

It was when Papa came home and they were sitting having their soup that Ayub finally came out with what was bothering him. 'Papa, are we Muslim?' he asked.

The soup went cold as Ayub told his parents about his day. About his days since the terrorist attacks in Mumbai. With the images of the Taj Hotel dome burning fresh in their minds, Ayub's classmates had started their teasing, taunting and yes, even bullying. Ayub recalled all that had been happening to him.

'"It's you guys who do this every time."

"Every time."

"You Mossies are just killers,"

"What d'you eat for breakfast? Bodies?"

"Do you drink blood instead of milk?"'

And then it had become worse. Shaan and his gang began teasing Ayub's friends, threatening them with dire consequences if they hung around with him anymore. Everytime they did, the others would pass by whispering, 'traitor', 'gadaar' 'khalnayak' ...

Eventually, only Shaurya had the guts to stick it out with Ayub.

'Just ignore them,' was his constant refrain.

But Ayub couldn't help tensing up every time there was another barb, another taunt, flung his way.

But that day it had crossed all boundaries. Shaurya wasn't in school that day, he'd gone for a tennis match. So Ayub was alone, he took his lunch box and tried to quickly go to the furthest corner of the playground. Get away before *they* could follow. But they'd seen him. Shaan had gathered his cronies and a whole lot of others who joined in. Many because they were too scared to say no to Shaan, but others because they too actually believed that all Muslims were, in fact, terrorists, or at least sympathisers to their cause. That had been the talk in their homes, often.

They waited for Ayub to disappear behind the trees that bordered the walls.

'Good,' smirked Shaan to himself.

In fact, Ayub had made it much worse for himself. He'd not managed to escape the gaze of his tormentors, but had gone to an isolated spot where no one would see what was happening to him.

As he sat, lunch box open, but not eating, they came for him.

'Ah Mossie boy, so here you are!'

'You planning to blow up the school or something?'

'Enjoying your blood sandwich, are you?'

One of them snatched the tiffin box from his hand and opened the sandwich. They jeered as it was crumbled and thrown to the ground. They cheered as one of them stamped on the box until it snapped and smashed. From the corner of his eye, Ayub saw that his cling-wrapped brownie had found its way into Shaan's pocket. Ayub tried to see if there was any escape for him. Could he make a dash for it? But there were too many of them. There was no way out.

No way out when Shaan caught hold of him from the back of his head. No way out when Shaan bent him over, rubbing his nose, his face into the ground. No way out as Ayub struggled for breath as he finally, finally sobbed out, as they demanded, 'I'm sorry, I'm sorry ... I am a Muslim ... I am a terrorist ... I'm sorry I killed so many people.'

The laughing and hooting subsided as they left him sobbing and dirty on the ground behind the trees. From far away, he'd heard the bell ring for the end of the break. But his legs were shaking too hard. He couldn't stand for a long time. Finally, he'd managed to struggle to the bathroom and wash his face. Not knowing what else to do. Knowing that there was no way he could go to the teachers and tell them what had just happened. That was out of the question. So he walked into class, late. Steeling himself for the inevitable taunting giggles that rose. And for the scolding for being late.

'Speak up! I'm asking you a question—why are you so late for class?'

He just let his head hang down, knowing that his silence was incensing the teacher more and more. But there was no answer he could give, so he mumbled a sorry and hoped it would be enough.

And then, through the afternoon, he was lost in thought, wondering how he was going to persuade his parents that he had to drop out of school, or at least transfer to another one. He took more scoldings for being inattentive in his stride. That was the least of his problems.

But most of all, Ayub just couldn't figure out

why they were picking on him. Was he different from all the others? And if yes, then, how?

Ayub added salty tears into the redness of his tomato soup. He couldn't bear it. He was the gentlest of children. He hated the way most boys would smack and knock each other 'just for the fun of it.' He couldn't see the fun in giving or receiving a painful whack.

He stayed clear of the rowdier boys and liked to play with the girls, although he couldn't do that too much, because then the teasing became worse, he explained.

'They say, we should kill all the Muslims and only then will the world be peaceful.'

'That's what they say?' Papa and Ma looked at each other, horrified.

They knew that they would one day talk about religion with their son, but they hadn't thought it would be so soon, when he was just ten years old. They came from different religions—he was Muslim and she was Christian. Neither family had accepted, or even forgiven them for falling in love. There had been bitter fights at their homes. Bordering on violence, almost.

No one from their families had attended the quiet court marriage that they'd had. They had never practiced their religions after that. 'If it causes so much hatred, what good is it to go through the motions of praying to pieces of paper or stone statues?' they'd said. So they brought up their son without a religion. They celebrated birthdays, but no religious festivals. If he wanted to play Holi, or light candles at Diwali or get presents from Santa, he did. But they hadn't talked about the religious significance of what he was doing or that they were festivals of different religions.

They'd known this day would come, but yet, they weren't prepared at all to face it. And they hadn't imagined it would be brought up in such harsh circumstances.

They sat him down between them. They brought out family albums. Long ago ones that had his parents each of them as children. Each of them showing the religion they were born into. 'This is a cross, beta, there is a story about how the Lord Jesus Christ was crucified on it because of his beliefs.'

'This is my first Eid, see how proud every one is. I was the first son.'

And they explained to him that officially he was half Muslim and half Christian. You have the best of two worlds you know.

But the questions still remained. Why was he being taunted? And what did being half and half make him?

And when they had said all that could be said about it, Ayub asked, 'So I am Christian and I am Muslim and that's ok? And I'm not going to be a killer am I?' and his very last question is what shook them the most, 'why didn't you ever tell me about my religion before, were you ashamed of it?'

Ayub's parents knew that they were going to have to do something about it. Although he begged them not to, they went to school. They talked with the class teacher, the principal and some others. They were horrified too at what had happened. Like many schools, this one had left the question of religion and discussion around it out of the curriculum. Out of the assembly prayers even, where they chose non-religious prayers for the general good of mankind. Policies they thought would be correct and healing and not bring about any conflict. But it hadn't turned out that way. At all.

The classes were addressed. The teachers thought it best to take a direct approach. Rather than just suspending the children, they wanted to try and convince them. Ayub's parents agreed. So now they stood before the class, the parents and teachers and principal together.

Ayub was nervous. Would his friends laugh? Would they be rude to him again? Or to his parents? Would they understand at all? Ayub's parents were worried too. Had they done the right thing in not talking about all of this earlier? Had they talked of it too soon? Would their son and his classmates really be able to comprehend all that they were about to say about such a complex thing as religion, and the similarities and differences? That religion only ever taught you to be a good human being? There was no religion that said you had to be a killer. There were bad people in any religion who killed and used their faith as an excuse.

And so therefore it didn't matter what religion you were born with. One or more. Or any, for that matter.

One by one, they all read passages from different holy books. The *Bible*, the *Koran*, the *Bhagvad Gita*, the *Upanishads*. They also talked about some of the difficulties they'd faced, being from different religions. About how they'd come to be so wary that, in fact, they'd never even shared with their own son what his religion was. That they celebrated festivals of all religions, but never talked about their religious significance, because they felt that it had started to breed violence and hatred in the world.

The class shifted uneasily. Shaan hung his head as others were glancing at him. He'd often picked on other kids, for all kinds of reasons. But he'd never had to face such a direct approach. He felt the reproach rise within him. For himself.

And he could barely believe his ears when Ayub's mother extended the invitation. He looked up to see her smile at him as she said, 'So, we'd like to invite all of you to an Eid party. It will be Ayub's first official Eid. Here are the cards. We'd be very happy if your parents came too. I do hope that all of you will come.'

~

Finally, Ayub was dressed in his new white kurta pyjama. He wore his thread skull cap and he said his morning prayer on his brand new prayer mat. Kneeling alongside his father, watching from the corner of his eye as he bent forward and laid his forehead on the mat, facing in the direction of Mecca.

Then he'd helped both his parents put the silver foil on the kheer, put raisins into the sevian. Put crisp notes of money into the new white envelopes for his friends' Eidi that he'd decorated himself.

And now it was time for the party to start.

When the first car drove up, Ayub felt almost faint with surprise, joy and terror. But his mother held his shoulder and gave him a small secret squeeze. They opened the door together to start celebrating Ayub's first Eid.

Afifa

Siddhartha Sarma

They say the prophet Daoud was so loved by Allah, He gave him a most special gift that He gave to none of the other thousands of prophets before and after him—music. His songs could bewitch animals of the forest, they say. This same Daoud, who once beat the giant Goliath with a slingstone, he could sing. I wish my Daoud were like him, but he isn't.

When my Daoud was born, Ammi says I saw him at the hospital and I smiled. She said I was so happy I had a little brother at last. Ammi says I loved Daoud more than she did. I was five, and I must have been insane.

Daoud's main purpose on being born was to make life miserable for me. Okay, you can say that for any little brother that ever infected his elder sister's life. You can say they are terrors when they are young, and as my aunt says, they embarrass you when they grow up. Nothing good ever came of a younger brother.

Before you start asking, they spelt his name that way because Abbu was in Tangier for a while and that's how they spell it there, and he liked it. Don't ask *me*.

When he was fourteen months and teething, he never bit anyone, except me. Ammi would carry him around and he would be a total angel, he would. But Ammi would say, 'Afifa, hold him for a bit' or something and he would bite my shoulder. No matter how much I screamed or how much Ammi pulled his legs, he would hang on. I tell you, he *liked* it.

When he started crawling, he would hide under a table and lunge to bite my ankles. I had little teeth-marks on my shoulders and ankles all those years. I swear. It was worse than having a dog in the house, but would my parents ever hear a word against him? Oh, no. It would always be, 'Afifa, he's so small!'

Now he isn't, he's nine. I have tried to train him to fetch and carry things for me. But he is cunning, oh yes he is. I tell him, 'Daoud, fetch my pen' and because Ammi will cuff him if he talks back these days, he fetches the pen.

I say, 'Daoud, why is the refill not inside it?'

He says, 'But you told me to fetch the pen, not the refill.' Then he grins that evil grin of his which he makes sure Ammi doesn't see.

Then I send him again to get the refill he has hidden somewhere. It means more work for him, but he doesn't mind so long as it pisses me off.

Alright, this was supposed to be about what a wonderful Eid I had today but it has become another page in my 'Why elder sisters will go to heaven' diary, or an account of the terror I live with.

Okay, I must think happy thoughts, but really, when you hear what happened today.

Eid-ul-fitr days are awesome. There is so much fun after a month of fasting, we have friends and people visiting. When my grandparents were here, they would tell the two of us about the real significance of Eid, about a celebration after fasting and such. For us it was fun.

But Daoud seizes this day as another chance to be mean to me.

Last year, when Abbu was at home, they dressed up to go to the mosque. You see, only men pray at the mosque with other men. Women pray at home. Daoud was kneaded into a new little kurta by Ammi and came out looking like a stuffed pillow, his hair brushed and neat. He was clearly uncomfortable because the kurta was starched and he doesn't like being neat and clean (as you may have guessed) but he hopped around me and said he was going to the mosque with Abbu and I couldn't come, which he knew made me sad because I like being with Abbu as much as I can.

This was the first Ramzaan I fasted with Ammi, for the whole month. It takes getting used to, except Daoud ate all the time just to make me feel even more hungry during the day, for the whole month. Evenings, when we broke the fast, it was good, except Abbu wasn't here.

He wasn't home today either, for Eid. He told Ammi on the phone a few days ago that he might not be able to reach on time because some work had come up. Eid is not the same without him.

We woke early this morning and said the *salah*, the special prayer on this day. Daoud had been feeling a little low with Abbu not here. I was feeling low too, but Daoud just likes showing off and getting hugged by Ammi, it's just like him.

Usually, Abbu and he would go to the graveyard with the other men to pray to the ancestors, but of course not this time. Ammi was to take us along to her sister's place down the road and help make the food and such for guests.

Daoud was lying in bed and Ammi went to tell him to get ready, but he was running a temperature. Ammi checked it and it was very high. I mean, he never gets sick. I think he ate some of those sweets from the fridge last night because I swear there were a lot of them the last I checked.

This put a crimp on the whole day, you know. It's just like him (oh, I said that already). If he is not having fun, he won't let me either.

'Afifa, you go on to your aunt's house. I will have to stay here with him,' Ammi said.

But, you know, I didn't want Ammi to miss out

on today. I mean, it's only once a year, and she really likes the festivities.

I told her maybe I could return in a bit and she could go to my aunt's while I stayed back with Daoud. I said, he was sure to get better and I would stay. Don't ask me why I said it. I just wanted Ammi to go out too. It's got absolutely nothing to do with Daoud.

Ammi smiled and there was something in her eye. She kissed my forehead and said what would she do without me.

Daoud opened his eyes and shot me an evil look.

He is a cunning, cunning fiend, I tell you.

At my aunt's I met the cousins and the neighbours and it was crowded and noisy and fun, but just not the same visiting alone. I almost wished Daoud was with me. Well, almost. Nobody should be alone on Eid, the first day of the month of Shawwal. Nobody should be left out when everyone else is having fun.

I returned home in a while and Ammi left but said I should call her immediately if Daoud needed anything. I checked his forehead, it was still hot and he was sleeping.

Oh, what a way for the day to go. My cousins were hogging on sweets and such and I was stuck with my idiot brother. He probably learnt to increase his body temperature on command or something, just to spite me.

Well, Afifa is not going to bend before such events. If I couldn't go have fun, I will have fun on my own.

I don't much like cooking. If you ask me to help you make the usual food, I might help, but it's not really interesting. Different kinds of dishes, now that's exciting. Ammi says I get it from Abbu: he can't cook to feed himself, but show him a new recipe, and he's beside himself.

I don't know of many people who cook *mrouziya* on Eid. My aunt doesn't, or at least she didn't till Abbu got this idea two years ago and got the ingredients from Tangier. It's very simple to make and I checked and saw we had everything I needed.

I got about a kilo of the lamb chunks Ammi had kept in the freezer and thawed it. Then I heated it in the microwave and coated it with this spice Abbu had got. It's called *ras-el-hanout*. It's the best part of the dish. It's got cardamom, cinnamon, clove, peppercorn, turmeric and many other things Abbu had mentioned but I forget, sorry. It's just awesome-tasting.

So, really carefully, I spread a couple of spoons of it on the lamb chunks. Then I added two cups of water like Abbu said, honey and olive oil. Then I baked it. The spice (oh I just remembered, it also has rosebud in it) starts smelling nice immediately. It was so much fun.

I got it out, kept it warm and removed the oil, then I took the lamb out. Abbu says this makes it taste better and the less the oil, the healthier it is. I put some raisins in and boiled the stew. Then I put the lamb back in and boiled it again.

There. I thought I'd keep it for Ammi, although I wished some guest would come, but by now Ammi would be gushing about how sick her Daoud was and people would be sorry for the little guy so they would not want to come and disturb him.

Even while he is sleeping, my brother messes with my life.

I went into his room. His eyes were closed and his hands were under his chin. If I didn't know his true nature, I would have said: 'Oh, what a cute little boy.' I bet he sleeps like that on purpose so Ammi will melt everytime she sees him.

I ate some of the *mrouziya* with white bread. You should have been there, you'd have loved it. Abbu would have loved it too.

I went back to Daoud's room. He was stirring, and his forehead was still warm. I shook him.

'Do you want to eat?' I asked.

He opened one eye, the way he does when he is planning something against me.

'When is Ammi coming back?'

'Soon. You want me to call her?'

He closed his eye and didn't say anything.

Oh. Is he really feeling bad or just pretending?

'Hey Daoud, are you hungry? I made some *mrouziya*.'

He opened an eye again and looked at me as if I had told him to have a bowl of Pedigree.

'Mmm-hmm.'

So I got him the lamb on a plate and fed little bits to him with white bread. He likes white bread. I wiped his mouth and tucked him in and he slept till Ammi returned.

Her eyes sparkled, I tell you, when she saw the

mrouziya and she hugged me and said I made everything worthwhile. She said it was delicious, but I knew that.

I didn't tell her I'd fed Daoud but he must have told her, in that complaining voice of his. I can never do anything right, that's what he usually thinks.

I sat at his side before coming to my room. He was feeling better, Ammi said. He opened his eyes and looked at me.

'I saw a dream,' he said.

'Mm-hmm.'

'I thought you were a frog.'

Okay, so you will say he was delirious or something, but what can you do with someone like that?

They say Eid means 'celebration'. Usually it is. But it is very difficult if you have my Daoud in your house. As I write he sleeps and dreams of me being a frog or something and tomorrow he will be better and might even try to eat my diary.

But, today, Ammi and I met the cousins, and we prayed for ourselves and for Abbu, and all our friends, even those who don't pray to Allah. And

Daoud ate the *mrouziya* I made and was too sick to make faces and claim I was poisoning him.

Abbu says to be thankful for small things.

The Goat Who Got Away

Samina Mishra

Ismail was a billy goat, the stud of the Zakir Nagar streets. A handsome, black and white goat with sharp curved horns, long black ears and a short black tail. His body was white with one large black patch running all the way from his chin down to his chest. He had an air of majesty about him and when he walked, the other goats made way for him. Someone had put a shiny garland of pink and green tinsel with an old CD in the centre around his neck and Ismail wore it proudly, as if it marked him out as the lucky one. And indeed, he seemed to be quite lucky in foraging for food. He always managed to get the choicest pieces of stale roti from Zakir Nagar's garbage dumps, old bits of rope and even leaves from the few bushes that had survived Zakir Nagar's construction boom. The fruit-sellers would hand him the overripe fruit that they knew wouldn't get sold and the housewives would leave out their vegetable peelings for him. None of the other goats would touch these until Ismail had had his share and moved on.

Ismail belonged to no one, no sir, he was very much his own person—or billy goat, as it were. It was more a case of Zakir Nagar belonging to him. There wasn't a goat on the streets that didn't know about him. Mother goats would point him out to their babies just as soon as they were able to stand without their knees buckling over. And the older goats who had missed coming under the butcher's knife because of their stringy muscles looked to him for a corner of the garbage dumps to call their own.

Now, if he didn't belong to anyone, didn't have an owner, then, you might ask, how did he get the name Ismail? After all, names are mostly given by others—parents, owners, people who have rights over a body. And the one who does the naming is the one who calls the shots, the one who has to be obeyed, right? Well, who had rights over Ismail? Who was he to obey? Now there's a story and I think it's time it was told.

Ismail was born to a nanny goat that belonged to an Imam in one of the local masjids. When he was a kid, he was a beautiful little thing, prancing around the masjid courtyard. The Imam was very fond of goat's milk and so, he would try and keep the kid away from the nanny goat until he'd had a chance to milk her. Mornings were easy because he'd just put a large basket over the sleeping kid and lead the nanny goat away but evening milking time was the Imam's wife's responsibility and there was much shouting and shoving and shushing, as the kid, who would become Ismail, knocked over things trying to get to his bleating mother.

Finally, the Imam who sat at one end of the courtyard conducting *Koran* classes for a group of children in the evenings, told the children to bring the kid to class. The children were more than happy to have this distraction in the midst of their *Alif-Laam-Meems*. They fought over whose turn it was to sit with the kid, played with its long black ears and fed it little tid-bits. The kid began to enjoy this attention and soon forgot about its mother. Five o'clock *Koran* class became his favourite time of day. He got to play with the children, sit among their books and sniff the pages, eat the smuggled treats and then, to top it all, listen to the end-of-class story that the Imam told the children. The stories were all from the *Koran*, about prophets and miracles and why Allah should be obeyed. It was the part of class that the children liked best and the kid sat among them, soaking up their enthusiasm. When their eyes widened in wonder, so did his. When their mouths hung open in amazement, so did his. And when they smiled, the kid nodded in appreciation, letting the bell around his neck tinkle gently. And so, many weeks passed and the kid-who-would-be-Ismail grew big and strong.

One evening, after the children had finished their *Koran* reading, the Imam decided to tell them the story of The Great Sacrifice. Eid-ul-Zoha or

Bakra Eid, as it was popularly called, was a week away and he thought it was time for the children to understand what the festival was all about. 'You all know about the Prophet Ibrahim,' he began, 'well, one day he received a message from Allah asking him to sacrifice what was dearest to him as a sign of his true faith. What was dearest to him was of course his son, Ismail, and Ibrahim didn't know what to do.' The Imam paused.

The children looked confused and the goat-who-would-be-Ismail looked at them uncertainly. Little Faizaan raised his hand and asked, 'But what does sacrifice mean, Imam sahib?' The Imam pulled at his beard thoughtfully, trying to find a way to explain this. 'Sacrifice ... it means giving up something that you value for something or someone that you think is more important. In this case, Allah. Allah is the most important, isn't he? And so, Ibrahim had to obey His command.' The goat-who-would-be-Ismail seemed to understand. He'd heard the Imam say Allah-o-Akbar countless times and explain to the children that it meant God is Great. He'd figured out that Allah was the one that everyone thought had rights over everything—

the masjid, the people, even the goats. He wasn't sure how it worked but he was willing to go along with it.

'But how was he to sacrifice Ismail?' asked Haaris. The Imam looked a little uncomfortable. 'He had to give him up to Allah, kill him,' he mumbled. The children took a quick in-drawn breath, in collective shock and the goat-who-would-be-Ismail widened his eyes in alarm. This business of the rights didn't seem ... well, quite right. 'Wait,' continued the Imam quickly and more forcefully, 'the story has a happy ending. You will see the miracle of Allah in the story. Ismail was unhurt. What happened was that when Ibrahim took him to the place of the sacrifice, he wept and said that he just couldn't do it. But Ismail, who was also a true believer, told him that Allah's command must be obeyed. He told his father to tie a blindfold over his eyes so he wouldn't have to see what he was doing while performing the sacrifice.'

The children sat up straight, waiting tensely to hear the rest. The goat-who-would-be-Ismail did too. 'So, that's what Ibrahim did. He brought down the knife while he was blindfolded and when he opened the blindfold, do you know what he saw?' The children leaned forward and shook their heads and the goat-who-would-be-Ismail did too. The Imam smiled, 'Ismail stood to one side, hale and hearty and on the spot of the sacrifice, with its head cut off lay a goat!' A goat! The goat-who-would-be-Ismail felt a ripple of shock run through his body. He couldn't believe what he had just heard. Happy ending, indeed! And what about the scapegoat in the great sacrifice?

The children began to chatter, oblivious to the goat's presence. He felt forgotten and forlorn. So, he stood up and before he even knew what he was going to do, he bolted. Right through the masjid's courtyard, out of the doorway and down the gali. He ran and he ran and he ran. He ran past honking cars, crowded shops, sleeping dogs, wailing babies. He ran through Zakir Nagar and Batla House, turned left at the end of the sloping road near the bus stop, slowed down as he went past Khalillulah Masjid and huffed his way down to the river.

The sun was setting as he reached the riverbank and the golden sunlight made the Yamuna look more picturesque than it actually was. The washermen were pulling their clothes off the lines and some young boys were playing cricket. The goat-who-would-be-Ismail flopped down near some bulrushes and breathed deeply. He looked out over the river and pondered. Was this a goat's life? He sighed.

The story ran through his head—Ibrahim, Allah, Ismail, the dearest thing ... Hang on a minute, thought the goat. The Dearest Thing. It has to be the dearest thing—not a goat! Hurrah! I'm safe, I'm not the dearest thing, thought the goat-who-would-be-Ismail, I'm safe. He got up and jiggled a little jig. But then his eyes fell on the dhobis nearby, loading their blinkered mules with the laundry and he sat down with a thud. He had figured out what the story meant but would the others?

Just then, the magreb azaan rang out—Allah o Akbar—and the goat thought, OK, ok, I heard you. I know who's calling the shots. But, if the great sacrifice doesn't have to be of a goat, then you've got to give me a way to prove it! An eagle circled overhead and the goat watched it. Large lazy circles turned into smaller, quicker ones and then it pounced. When it rose up again, the goat could see a flat, shiny object held in its talons. The eagle flew closer and then released the object which was clearly not food. It spiralled downwards, towards the goat and before he could get up and out of its path, thud, it fell straight onto the goat's right horn. It was a disc and the centre had gone neatly through the tip of the horn and now sat like Saturn's ring around it. The goat-who-would-be-Ismail was not pleased. He shook his head and nodded vigorously but the disc was stuck. This is just not my day, he thought, and turned woefully towards Zakir Nagar.

When he arrived at the masjid courtyard, the Imam started shouting. Two of the boys from the *Koran* class were still there and they came forward to help. 'Look, he's got a CD stuck on his horn,' said Faizaan and started to laugh. The goat-who-would-be-Ismail hung his head sadly. 'Let's pull it off and find out what it is,' said Haaris. So, with the Imam holding the goat, the two boys tugged the CD off carefully. The Imam kept grumbling through the proceedings but once the disc was off, he grabbed it and told the boys to call Abu Bakr from the computer shop next door.

Abu Bakr arrived and when the Imam showed him the CD, he went back to his shop and returned with a battered laptop computer. 'It's probably too damaged to play,' he said. The CD was inserted and the computer groaned and moaned but managed to read it. 'Lucky,' said Abu Bakr as he double clicked on the CD icon. The Imam and the boys crowded around to see what would play and the curious goat-who-would-be-Ismail stayed on the fringes. An image popped up on the screen of a man with a flowing beard sitting on a dais with a mike in front of him. He began to speak. 'Today I shall speak about sacrifice. Qurbaani.' The Imam's eyes widened. 'Buuuutttt . . . That's just what I did some time ago,' he squeaked.

The goat-who-would-be-Ismail couldn't believe his ears, for the second time that day. 'I, Mulla Nasiruddin, will point out what true sacrifice is all about,' continued the image on the screen, 'sacrifice is about giving up something you love, something that is important to you. But today, people have forgotten that and when they are asked to sacrifice, they find the nearest animal—a sheep, a goat, a camel—and the killing of that creature is the qurbaani. Tell me, is that the thing dearest to you?' The Imam and the goat stood transfixed, both with their own thoughts running wild.

The image began to pixillate. 'I think not,' thundered the voice and then suddenly the image froze. Abu Bakr tried to quit it, play it, restart it but nothing seemed to work. Meanwhile, the Imam was in a bit of a daze. 'It is a divine coincidence, a divine coincidence,' he muttered. Faizaan and Haaris turned to the goat-who-would-be-Ismail and declared, 'Then, Imam Sahib, you have to thank him. He is the one who brought the CD.' The goat, almost as dazed as the Imam, looked quizzically at the group. Abu Bakr shut down the computer, ejected the CD and handed it over to the Imam. 'The boys are right, Imam sahib,' he laughed, 'so, how are you going to thank the goat—not make him part of the great sacrifice?!'

The Imam looked at him thoughtfully, 'Perhaps, you're right,' he muttered. 'Yes, yes, yes!' shouted the boys. Yes, yes, yes? thought the goat-who-would-be-Ismail. He couldn't believe his ears for the third time that day. But when the boys approached him with a garland of shining tinsel, he threw back his head and let them put it around his neck. The boys paraded him down Zakir Nagar's streets telling everyone the story. People came out of their homes and stopped their work to listen. Some people gave the goat food, others patted him, still others felt his horns. And at the end, someone managed to thread the CD onto the garland and the goat felt like he'd been crowned a king.

At night, as he lay down to sleep, he thought: I'm the one who got away, I'm not the goat in the story. I'm Ismail. And so, that's how the goat-who-would-be-Ismail came to be called Ismail. At least in his own mind—and that's the only one that counts, right?

Badi Ammi

Lovleen Misra

It was Eidi time of the year. This was the second most wonderful time of the year for Hameeda and her brother Hamza (the first being their respective birthdays). It was also the one time when they could tease Badi Ammi unashamedly. They called it the 'fight for their rights'!

Badi Ammi was really stubborn about the kids' Eidi. She insisted on giving ONLY one rupee as Eidi to Hameeda and her brother, Hamza. While the price of petrol, milk, school fees, chocolates, toys and movie tickets had gone up by leaps and bounds, Badi Ammi's Eidi stayed where it had started—at one rupee.

Badi Ammi was Hameeda's Ammi's Ammi, or to put it simply, her maternal grandmother.

The funny thing about Badi Ammi's Eidi was that she gave it with such fanfare, hugs and kisses that one would have thought a gold or a silver coin was being given. Quite early in the morning on Eid, Badi Ammi, having bathed and done her Namaaz, would call out to all the children excitedly, 'Which of you wish to be Allah Miyaan's Farishtey? There is lots of Eidi waiting for you ... whoever comes first gets the most! So come soon!' Waves of hope would surge through Hameeda and Hamza's hearts at this call, but alas, what they were handed was always just a shining coin.

As Hameeda braided her hair into a stylish, four-rope, intricate plait, her Ammi rushed into their room, 'Hami! Hamzu! Can't you hurry and get ready? Badi Ammi has been calling out for you for the last half-an-hour!'

Hamza, lost in the latest Playstation, surfaced to remark, 'Why hurry for chewing gum money?'

Hameeda could not agree more with her thirteen-year-brother. 'Really, ammi! Every year we beg, plead and cry in front of her but she just refuses to be generous.'

'That's not the way to talk about your elders, especially Badi Ammi,' Ammi said. 'She came to live with us for you both. She'd give up the world for you two thankless devils, while you two ...! Now come on, enough hairstyling, Hami! Get up, Hamzu!'

Hameeda and Hamza dragged their feet to Badi Ammi's bedroom. Just as they neared Badi Ammi's room, they heard her counting, 'Two-fifty ... three hundred ... fifty ... hundred and another fifty! Wah! That adds up to exactly five hundred.'

Hameeda and Hamzu's eyes lit up and they did a quiet and jubilant high five. Perhaps this Eid, Allah had heard their prayers and 'reformed' Badi Ammi. Finally, the one rupee was on its way out. Hameeda stopped Hamza at the door. 'Ssh! Let's wait a bit, Hamzu. Maybe she has more money to count out for us?'

Hamza shook his head in agreement and the two of them hid behind Badi Ammi's lovely dhakai print curtains. There was pin-drop silence inside her room. Hameeda was now absolutely sure Badi Ammi had saved lots of money for them which she was counting carefully and quietly. Hameeda was already daydreaming on how she would spend her 1000 rupees ... Should she buy a party dress? Or firecrackers for Diwali, just ten days away? Or that new Barbie Design Studio they were advertising on all the cartoon channels? Her dreams ended suddenly when someone shoved her.

Hamza, sweating profusely, had flung the curtain to one side. 'Hami! I'll die if I stay behind this sack. She must have finished counting. Let's go!'

Triumphant smiles plastered across their faces, they leaped into Badi Ammi's room.

'Eid Mubarak, Badi Ammi!'

Badi Ammi was surrounded by Jamuna Bai and Bholu's three children. She was asking them what they planned to do with their Eidi. The trio was giggling in reply.

Hameeda saw Jamuna Bai, the lady who helped Ammi in her housework, standing quietly aside. Bholu was trying to get his children to touch Badi Ammi's feet in the correct way. Bholu was Hameeda's Abbu's office helper and had been working at Abbu's office since he was seventeen. His children were thrilled to hold the crisp new hundred rupee notes.

'Here Jamuna and Bholu, come here and take your Eidi . . . come, come! You are my children too.'

And another two crisp and new hundred rupee notes were given to Jamuna Bai and Bholu, who touched Badi Ammi's feet reverentially.

Hamza whispered quickly into Hami's ear, 'If they are getting hundred, we'll surely get one thousand!' Hameeda's face lit up and she exhaled loudly in expectation.

Badi Ammi noticed the two now. 'Ah! My angels! Eid Mubarak! I've been waiting for my two eyes to come. Wish me!'

And she hugged the two of them tightly. Badi Ammi's kisses had a lovely betel leaf flavour to them. And her hugs carried a fragrance of the attar she wore. She had worn Hameeda's favourite sandalwood attar today. Badi Ammi slid the familiar piece of metal into their pockets. *'Kullu am wa antum bi khair,'* Badi Ammi said in Arabic, which meant: 'May you be well throughout the year!'

Neither Hamza nor Hameeda realised that the Eidi had been given. For a moment the two looked longingly at Badi Ammi. They knew it would be too rude to 'ask' for it. Badi Ammi smiled naughtily at the children. Both looked at each other.

Badi Ammi broke the silence. 'Kabir says God is inside, don't go looking for him anywhere.' Hamza shook his head impatiently. Badi Ammi continued, 'The Eidi is inside your pockets my darlings! Go on, look at it!'

The two of them went berserk emptying out their front, back, and wherever-else pockets. And there it was—Badi Ammi's famous one rupee coin.

Badi Ammi knew what would follow.

Hamza angrily thrust the coin back into her hand. 'What is this, Badi Ammi? Again one rupee? You can't even get a cycle puncture fixed with one rupee! Which world do you live in? Every year it's the same! I don't want it!'

'And we know, Badi Ammi, you gave more Eidi to Bholu's children. And Bachoo told me you've promised to give him a muffler and a pair of socks for Eid,' Hameeda shouted. 'I've decided: I am not eating anything till you give me more money. And ... and ... if you still don't, I'll stop sleeping with you at night. Then you'll know!'

Badi Ammi, unmoved by it, asked, 'Achha? And you, Hamza, what's your plan?'

Hamza marched to Badi Ammi's antique chest of drawers and grabbed Hameeda's Ludo board and Uno card game that were kept on it. He held them tight and announced, 'We are going to stop playing with you. And please don't ask me to dig out your chappals from under the bed. Or to find your spectacles!'

Badi Ammi was cool. 'Is that all, or any more threats?'

Hameeda climbed on to Badi Ammi's old rosewood arm chair. From being a protest movement it was turning into a revolution. She held Badi Ammi's specs in her hand, like a revolutionary flag. She proclaimed, 'No more one rupee! Pay up or your spectacles are ours forever!'

She tossed the pair of spectacles to Hamza, who caught it effortlessly.

Badi Ammi clapped, 'Good catch! Now I know whom to get my glasses from.'

Hamza threw the specs back to Hameeda. Ammi entered the camphor-fragrant room just at that moment, and she was livid.

'Grow up, you two!' She took the glasses from Hami and wiped them carefully on her dupatta.

'It's not the money but the love and *dua* of Badi Ammi that matters. You have a grandmother who lives with and for you. Isn't that a great gift?'

Badi Ammi motioned to Ammi to calm down. 'Sorry, my angels. One rupee is all that your poor Badi Ammi can afford. In my time we didn't get even this much. As for Bachoo, he needed a muffler and a pair of socks very badly. By Allah's grace, you both have all the comforts of life, and may it always be so.'

'You two are my eyes, how can my eyes be angry with me?' She ruffled their hair and pinched the cheeks on their frowning faces. 'And by the way, have you found your gifts as yet? Your first clue is in the direction of Mecca. It is kept on a piece of furniture out there ...'

'In the direction of Mecca? Furniture?' Hameeda asked, scratching her head.

'Mecca means west. That means the living room and furniture means the sofa, stupid!' Hamza said in a rush. 'So Bad-mi means the first clue is on the sofa!'

Before Badi Ammi could finish laughing, the two had shot off to find the first clue to their hidden gifts. And the one rupee revolution died a natural death.

~

As always, Badi Ammi had made a treasure hunt of their Eid gift-giving. She would supply them with clues in serial order, which would send the children meandering from one corner of the house to another, like Columbus went when he set sail for America. The clues would be mildly cryptic, involving characters and places from the stories she told them at bedtime. These were stories from the life of the Prophet, stories from the *Bible*, tales of Mulla Nasruddin, Tenali Raman, Akbar and Birbal, and of Queens and Emperors.

Badi Ammi's voice had grown quite weak over the years. Of late, a nagging cough also troubled her, but she never missed the daily story-telling session. Lying next to her each night, on her clean, pure white bedsheet, her breath smelling of lovely elaichi-laung, and playing with her soft, muslin, attar-laden dupatta, they were mesmerised by these stories. They hardly realised when they had drifted off to sleep and entered their own world of stories.

The treasure hunt over, Hameeda and Hamzu excitedly unwrapped their gifts. This year, like every year since they had learnt reading, Badi Ammi had gifted them storybooks. Hamza was given the tales of Amir Hamza, and Hameeda, a collection of Sheikh Chilli stories.

Hamza rushed into Badi Ammi's arms, 'Shukriya, Badi Ammi!'

Hameeda excitedly flipped through the pages of Sheikh Chilli. 'Thank you, Badi-mi!' she smiled happily. 'See Hamzu, it even has the story she told us last night—when Sheikh Chilli thinks he has fooled the King when actually it's he who has been fooled ...'

Suddenly Hamza, very concerned, asked, 'But when did you go and get these books? You can hardly walk till the door with that bad knee.'

Badi Ammi was quiet. Hameeda answered, 'I know!' She circled her Sheikh Chilli book in the air and said, 'Abracadabra gilli gilli chhoo! Farishta Jibril! Get me these books for Hami and Hamzu, before Eid!'

Badi Ammi nodded her head in agreement. 'Wah,

Hami! And this magic costs me only one rupee!'

Hameeda and Hamzu exclaimed together, 'One rupee?'

'Yes, just one rupee. It takes one rupee to call the bookstore and place the order. The books are delivered home. You can still do some good things with one rupee.'

'But the books couldn't be costing one rupee?' Hameeda quizzed, searching the back of the book for its price.

'Ya Khuda! What is with you twenty-first century children? There is a world where money and material things don't matter. Not when it's to do with loved ones! Now run along, your sheer korma is waiting for you.'

Badi Ammi's sheer korma was legendary. No one made it the way she did. Hameeda dashed to the dining room. But Hamza was not one to give up easily. On the way out he muttered, 'Remember . . . next Eid, one rupee won't do!'

'That is if I am around next Eid, Hamza Hussain,' Badi Ammi sighed to the empty room.

~

The next morning at nine, Badi Ammi came into the garden to sit in her old carved wrought-iron chair. On foggy winter mornings or on rainy days, she would sit in the front veranda, but in pleasant weather, it was the lawn for her.

While she watched the casuarina, gulmohur and other fruit trees gently sway in the cool September breeze, Bachoo brought her customary ginger tea with a few biscuits. Bachoo was their gardener and night watchman. He could identify a tree just by smelling and feeling its leaves in the dark.

After serving her tea, he sat on the ground close to her chair. He looked fondly at his new woollen socks. They were his Eid gift from Badi Ammi. 'Nani memsaab, even at this age you have such a sharp memory. You actually remembered that last winter a mouse nibbled away my socks. God bless you, Nani memsaab.'

Badi Ammi smiled, 'The cold gets in easily through the feet . . .' And she took a sip of the tea.

Hameeda had come out into the garden to call Bachoo. But for some reason she chose to quietly listen to Badi Ammi and Bachoo's conversation.

'Bachoo, you see that Papaya tree there?'

Bachoo nodded his head. '*Jee*, Nani memsaab. I remember you planted it for Hamza when he was three years old.'

Badi Ammi smiled at Bachoo's ability to remember such small facts. 'Yes, that was the first time he had tasted papaya.'

The irritating cough started and Badi Ammi became breathless. She took quick sips of the ginger tea. It helped. 'You know, Bachoo, ripe papayas bruise easily and won't last long. When I look at them, it reminds me of my present state. If all goes well, maybe a year or two more, and then ...'

Bachoo cut in before Badi Ammi could go any further. 'Don't talk like that Nani Memsaab!' He took a small brown packet out of his shirt pocket. 'A small gift for you, on Eid, from my village. The Hakim says this Unani powder mixed with honey will cure your cough in just two weeks.'

Badi Ammi stroked Bachoo's head and said, 'Bless you, my son. To be sensitive towards others is a priceless treasure. Never lose it.'

A gentle breeze blew through the garden swaying the slender branches of the guava, custard apple and pomegranate trees. Hameeda, leaning against the aadu tree, listened silently to Badi Ammi's conversation.

Suddenly something fell with a loud thump. Badi Ammi looked around. Hameeda hurriedly bent down to pick it up.

'What's that you've got, Hami?' Badi Ammi called out in her deep voice. Hameeda came forward to kneel before Badi Ammi. She showed her her gullak, a little piggy bank made of terracotta.

'Abbu gave this to me. He says I can begin saving some of my Eidi in this and then next Eid, break it open to see how much I've collected.'

'Yes, and then you can lend me some,' Badi Ammi said, teasingly.

Hameeda, not to be outdone, retorted, 'No, no, Badi Ammi, I've decided to put only the one rupee coins you give me every Eid in it. But if you help me fill it up *before* Eid, then maybe I could lend you some.'

'Tough luck, jaan. One rupee is what you always get and always will. I could, of course, put some magic *dua* in it so that this gullak may always be brimming with money and good luck!' Saying this,

Badi Ammi took out a bit of the Unani powder Bachoo had given her. She sprinkled some in the gullak through its slit.

'Wow, Badi Ammi! Is your cough medicine good for making money grow? Can I have more, to keep in my toy and clothes drawers?'

Badi Ammi and Bachoo looked at each other. 'No, it's for everyone. A little magic in our lives is good, but too much might be boring!' Badi Ammi folded the packet and rose from her chair. Hameeda helped Badi Ammi go back inside.

~

A few months later, Badi Ammi fell terribly ill. The cough had turned into a chest infection and soon her lungs too were infected. The doctors saw little hope of recovery, but tried, nevertheless.

Hameeda and Hamza would visit Badi Ammi in hospital every day after school. Hameeda would carry her magic gullak secretly tucked into her bag. She'd decided that the growing magic might heal her grandmother, but she knew that she couldn't tell anybody, but Badi Ammi, this.

When she caressed her grandmother's soft white hair, Badi Ammi would give her a weak wink. It was their secret, that gullak, and Hami knew that it made Badi Ammi feel better to have it around. Or maybe to have her and Hamza playing Ludo and Uno by her bed.

Badi Ammi died two days before Eid, in hospital.

Wiping a tear from her eye, Ammi told Hameeda and Hamza that Badi Ammi had left their Eidi for them. She handed them an envelope on which she had written in her beautiful handwriting:

Kullu am wa antum bi khair.
In giving to others, you give to yourself . . . Keep giving.
May Allah always be with you.

Azeeza's First Fast

Rukhsana Khan

Azeeza and her father climbed all the way to the roof of their apartment building. They came up twice a year, at the beginning and end of the month of Ramadan.

If the new moon was to be seen, it would be right above the glowing spot where the sun was disappearing.

Azeeza saw it first, a thin curved line in the rosy brightness of the sky. Like angels had taken a piece of white chalk and drawn a 'C', only backwards.

Azeeza pointed. 'Look father. Ramadan Mubarak! Tomorrow we will fast.'

Her father smiled. 'You're too young. Maybe next year.'

'I can do it.'

'It's a long time to go without eating or drinking. And you have to wake up early.'

'I can do it. I might even fast every day like you.'

'We'll see.'

When they went back down to their apartment, Azeeza's mother was waiting. Azeeza said, 'We're fasting tomorrow, Ummi. It's Ramadan!'

'Let her try,' said her father.

Azeeza's mother looked doubtful, but agreed.

That night Azeeza went to bed early, but it was hard to sleep. She'd show them. Before she knew it, someone was shaking her shoulder. It was still dark. She was still tired. 'Go away,' she muttered. 'I want to sleep.'

Her father bent down and whispered, his warm breath tickling Azeeza's ear. 'If you want to fast, you have to wake up for Suhoor.'

Azeeza's eyes flew open. She jumped out of bed and ran to the kitchen. Her mother was setting the table. 'Come and eat,' she said.

Azeeza looked at the food on the table and yawned. 'I'm not hungry.'

Her father picked her up and set her on the chair. 'You'll need your strength.'

Azeeza had a banana and half a bowl of cereal. Her mother frowned, looking worried. 'Eat some more. You'll get hungry.'

Azeeza wrinkled her nose.

'Fine then, drink some hot chocolate. But hurry. It's almost time to stop eating.'

Azeeza was finishing the last dregs of chocolate in the bottom of the cup when her father glanced at the clock and said, 'It's time to start fasting.'

Then they went to pray Fajr. During the prayer Azeeza yawned eight times. Afterward, her father kissed her and sent her back to bed.

When she woke up again, she changed her clothes, brushed her teeth (making sure not to swallow anything) and was off to school. This fasting was easy, she thought. It sure saved time.

At recess, she grinned while walking past the line at the water fountain. After recess, her mouth was a little dry, but she felt okay.

But during math, her stomach growled so loudly that the whole class heard.

'What was that?' cried Tony.

Azeeza wriggled in her seat. Were you supposed to say 'excuse me' if your stomach growled?

When it was lunchtime, she walked slowly home. She felt tired, and her stomach kept reminding her how empty it was.

Her mother met her at the door. 'How is your fast?'

'Okay, I guess.'

'Lie down. It's good to rest when you're fasting.'

Dropping her jacket, Azeeza went to the sofa. That's when she saw the jelly bean on the floor. Red, her favourite. Before she knew it, she'd popped it into her mouth. Mmm. Sweet and juicy. After she had swallowed, she remembered she was fasting.

'Oh no!'

Her mother came running. 'What's the matter? Are you all right?'

'It was an accident. I didn't mean to. Honest. I forgot. I found a jelly bean ...'

Her mother was smiling. 'That's okay, dear. You haven't broken your fast.'

'But I ate it.'

'It's okay if you forget and eat something. Allah

was the one who gave you the food anyway. But you have to stop eating when you remember. Did you do that?'

Azeeza nodded.

'Just try to remember next time, okay?'

'Okay.' She lay down on the sofa and dozed off. When she woke up, she felt a little thirsty but much better.

After she had prayed Zuhr she ran off to school.

But that afternoon there was a problem. Tony's mother brought in a chocolate birthday cake with sprinkles, to share with the class.

'Don't you want any?' asked the teacher.

Azeeza didn't answer.

Tony said, 'It's okay. She didn't put any pig stuff in it. I told her you can't eat pig stuff.'

'It's not that,' said Azeeza. 'I'm fasting.'

'What's that?'

She told the class.

Tony said, 'Go ahead and eat it. I won't tell. Neither will anyone else. Right?'

'Right,' said the others.

Azeeza shook her head quickly. 'Oh, no. I couldn't.'

'Why not?' asked one girl.
'Aren't you hungry?' asked another.
'Yes.'
'Then eat it.'
Azeeza looked down. 'I just can't.'
The teacher said, 'I have an idea. I'll wrap up your piece. Take it home and have it when you're finished fasting.'
'Oh, yes,' cried Azeeza. 'Thanks, Tony.'
Azeeza tucked the cake in her coat pocket. She wanted to take a lick of the chocolate icing, but she didn't. She even wished she could forget she was fasting, just for a moment, long enough to take a bite, but she didn't.

At recess, she played dodgeball. When she came in, she was so thirsty she raced to the water fountain. She took a big mouthful of ice cold water but remembered and spat it out. Her throat was still dry. She turned and marched into the classroom, looking back only once.

But by 4 p.m., as she trudged home tired and thirsty and hungry, she knew she couldn't make it. She didn't want to fast anymore. She had to eat. She had to drink. She wanted to eat the piece of cake in her pocket. She told her mother this as she helped her off with her coat.

'But it's not very long now. Only an hour and a half left.'

Azeeza slipped to the floor. 'But that's so long. I can't wait.'

Her mother led her to the sofa. 'You've fasted all day, it's a shame to quit now. Let's pray Asr and then you can rest. Read a book. The time will go by before you know it.'

After they had prayed Asr, Azeeza flopped down on the sofa. She didn't feel like reading. She felt like eating. Picking up a book, she got as far as the goodies Little Red Riding Hood was taking to Grandma's house when she remembered how hungry she was and threw the book down. Still an hour and fifteen minutes to go. Azeeza turned on the TV. There was a commercial for ice cream, then one for cereal and one for hamburgers. She shut off the TV.

Her stomach growled even louder.

In the kitchen, her mother was making pizza. The smell made Azeeza's mouth water.

Her mother looked up, 'I made it especially for you.'

Azeeza smiled weakly. 'I can't wait.'

'You're almost there.'

'It's so hard. Why do they call it fasting when it goes so slow?'

Her mother laughed. 'It's just the name for it, dear.'

'Why do we have to fast anyway?'

'It makes you feel lucky.'

Azeeza grumbled, 'I don't feel lucky.'

'Oh, but you are. When you've finished fasting, you can eat. Some poor people can't.'

Azeeza was quiet, watching her mother put the pizza in the oven.

Her father came in. 'Are you still fasting?'

Azeeza nodded.

Her father gave her a big hug. 'I'm proud of you. You're such a big girl.'

Yes, she was. A little girl couldn't have fasted the whole day.

'Go wash up. It's almost time to break the fast.'

Azeeza ran and washed her hands.

Her mother called, 'It's time.'

Azeeza grabbed her piece of cake from her coat pocket and galloped for the table.

'Slow down,' her mother cried. 'Don't eat too fast. You'll get sick.'

The sky was getting dark. They said the dua.

They said: 'O God, I believe in you and have fasted for Your sake. I put my trust in You. And I break my fast with food You gave me.'

Azeeza took a bite of a date. It was sweet and chewy and delicious. Then she took a bite of cake. It was also sweet and chewy and delicious. She drank a big glass of water and thought she'd never tasted anything as good.

Then they went to pray Maghrib. Azeeza couldn't wait till they were done and could eat supper.

When the pizza came, she thought she could eat the whole thing by herself. But after two pieces she was full.

Her father said, 'So, should I wake you up to fast tomorrow?'

Azeeza thought for a moment. 'Maybe not tomorrow, but the next day for sure.'

Azeeza fasted for four whole days over the month of Ramadan. Her dad fasted all of them, and her mother did most of them. Before she knew it, twenty-nine days had gone by, and they were climbing the stairs of the apartment building again, all the way to the roof.

If the new moon was to be seen, it would be right above the glowing spot where the sun was disappearing.

Azeeza saw it first, a thin curved line in the rosy brightness of the sky. Like angels had taken a piece of white chalk and drawn a 'C', only backwards.

Azeeza pointed. 'Look, fasting is finished. Tomorrow is Eid-ul-Fitr. Eid Mubarak!'

Sweets for Shankar

Adithi Rao

Bapu, he whispered. Eat something.
Bapu couldn't hear him. For he was many miles away, lying in a little bed, his life slipping away. Only his spirit remained strong, so strong...

~

Ashu wanted a doll. She had begged for one for so long now, and Munna badly wanted to get it for her.
'I stopped by Basha Bhai's toy shop on my way home yesterday to check the price. The doll you like costs six rupees!'

'Allah!' gasped Ashu, her eyes wide as saucers. 'So much!'

Then her longing got the better of her and she dropped her eyes and mumbled, 'But it's so beautiful.'

Munna's face softened. He decided to earn the money, no matter how long it took. He worked as an assistant in a shoe store after school each day, for which Kapoor Sahib paid him three rupees a month.

At Kapoor, Chand & Sons, Munna was the junior assistant. He hardly saw the customers who came and went, for his job was to remain up in the attic and throw down shoes of different sizes that the senior assistants yelled for, as they fitted out the customers. Clients. Kapoor Sahib insisted that they be called clients.

In the attic were hundreds of shoe boxes piled one over the other. At twelve years of age, Munna and Shankar, the other junior assistant, were the only ones small enough to move around with some ease in that confined space upstairs. So they ruled their territory like young lords, arranging everything according to some brilliantly devised system known unto them alone, that ensured that they never took more than a minute to find any pair of shoes in the size and colour that was needed below.

Munna liked his life at Kapoor, Chand & Sons. He liked Kapoor Sahib, who was always jolly and friendly. He liked the senior assistants who teased and laughed and made funny comments on the custo... *clients*, that came and went each day. Most of all, he liked Shankar, his simple little friend and co-worker.

This was Munna's life. School by day, the store every evening, home at night. At first Rafi Muhammed, Munna's father, had been displeased at the thought of his young son working. But times were getting harder, and money dearer. They needed Munna's three rupees to pay for their monthly ration of sugar. For some months now, Rafi's vegetable stall in the market place had become less and less lucrative. The ladies of the fine homes who once came to him, smiling and chatting easily as he picked out the freshest of peas and turai to fill their baskets, now walked quickly past his stall with lowered eyes, on to Bijoy Babu's cubbyhole next door where the vegetables were less green.

Only the women from the mohallas came to his shop anymore, their heads and faces covered. But they were so poor that they could just barely afford to buy their vegetables by the quarter kilo at a time. Sometimes, moved by the weariness in some woman's face, Rafi Bhai would throw in a few extra bhindis for free, tipping the weighing scale past the pau kilo mark.

Rafi realised that Munna was happy at Kapoor, Chand & Sons. The boy laughed there, he had friends there . . . In times like these, thought Rafi, even that is a lot.

One day, up in the attic, Munna and Shankar were taking a tea break.

'I've worked it all out,' said Munna. 'I'll give Abba rupees 2.50 from my salary and keep fifty paise each month. In about a year I'll have the money saved up to buy Ashu's doll.'

Shankar looked worried. 'But how will they manage at your home without the fifty paise?'

'Arrey, I drink so much tea that most of the sugar ration goes on me only! So I figured that if I stop taking sugar in my tea then that will make up for it. Isn't that a good idea?'

Shankar's large, innocent eyes lit up slowly. 'Yes, it really is. And Aisha will be so happy with her doll!'

Munna thought of his sister's delight and his heart clenched in anticipation of the happy day he'd surprise her with that much-coveted toy.

'What would you do if you were allowed to keep your earnings, Shankar?' asked Munna, seeing the far-away expression on the other boy's face. It was easy to talk about it because they both knew that such a thing would never happen. Shankar's family was too poor to spare a single paise on anything other than food.

Shankar thought for a long time. Munna didn't interrupt him because he knew this took some serious consideration.

'Maybe he'll buy himself a shirt,' mused Munna silently, as he watched the emotions play across the other boy's face. 'His are almost completely worn out ...'

'Pink sweets!' cried Shankar, his eyes shining.

'What?'

'I'd buy a dozen of those pink sweets from Anthony's bakery, and all of us at home would eat one. Not share, but eat one whole one each!'

'Those syrupy ones?' laughed Munna thoughtlessly. 'They are terrible.'

Shankar turned his head quickly and Munna's laughter faded. Their eyes held for a moment. Then Munna nodded awkwardly and looked away. In times like this, you did not mess with people's dreams.

Months passed and the New Year came around again. Life went on as usual in Munna's little world, but out there, great changes were taking place. They didn't matter too much to Munna, who was content and secure in his life of work and school. He had now managed to save two rupees of the six that he needed for Ashu's doll. He had even started to enjoy his tea without sugar!

Often on his way from the school to the store, Munna stopped by Basha Bhai's toy store to gaze at the doll. Ashu's Doll, he called it.

Then one day in July, something unexpected happened. Kapoor Sahib called Munna to him.

'Munna,' he said quietly. 'Take this money.'

Munna's eyes went from the six rupees to Kapoor Sahib's face. He frowned, puzzled.

'But it is not pay day, Sir. And so much money . . .?'

'It's this month's salary and the next. Here, keep it. Don't come back to work from tomorrow.'

Munna stared at Kapoor Sahib in shock.

'Have I done something . . .?'

'No, no, nothing! You're a good boy! A good . . .' his voice broke and he turned away. Munna looked around at the others, bewildered. Sumanth and Haresh didn't meet his eyes. Shankar was crying quietly in the corner. Munna couldn't understand it. What had happened in the course of these last few hours?

'Sir!' he cried desperately, and Kapoor Sahib turned around. Slowly some of the anguish from the older man's face melted and he pulled himself together. In a calmer voice he said, 'Beta, it is not safe now. That's why I don't want you to come back to work. If things settle down in time you'll have your old job back, I promise. But for a while you must remain at home. Now wait here at the store until it is night, and I will drop you home myself.'

Munna nodded and turned away, the six rupees clutched in his sweaty fist.

'And Munna?'

'Hmm?'

'Take off your skull cap.'

Munna and Shankar spent the rest of the afternoon huddled in the attic together. No more clients came in, for the shutter to the store's main entrance had been lowered and locked. All around there was a deathly calm that struck a note of terror in Munna's heart, although he couldn't entirely comprehend why.

As the hours ticked by, Munna slowly began to feel the fear loosen its grip over his heart. He spread out the damp and crumpled six rupee notes on the floor beside him to dry. Then he gazed at them thoughtfully, as if seeing them for the first time. Speaking in a low tone, he said, 'I already had two rupees saved up. With these six I have a total of eight.'

Understanding dawned on both boys at the same time. They sat up and grinned at each other excitedly.

'You can buy the doll for Aisha!' said Shankar happily.

Munna nodded, his eyes shining.

The two boys whispered the next three hours

away, talking about Aisha's surprise, making plans to meet outside work, reassuring each other, but really themselves, that nothing would change for their friendship. How hard would it be, really? After all, Munna lived in one of the mohallas of Raja Bazaar, and Shankar in Belighata, just a short distance away ...

The clock struck eight and Kapoor Sahib called to Munna from down below. The boys stopped speaking abruptly and looked at each other. Tears sprung to Shankar's eyes again, and suddenly Munna felt that he couldn't stand it. Blinking hard, he said gruffly, 'Allah hafiz.' Then he swung himself out through the opening in the attic and descended the ladder. Haresh and Sumanth patted his shoulder awkwardly as he walked past them and followed Kapoor Sahib out through the back door of Kapoor, Chand & Sons.

Kapoor Sahib led Munna to his car that was parked in the sheltered premises of the next door mechanic shop. It was an old Fiat, a 1930 model. Munna moved to open the gate when Kapoor Sahib snapped tensely, 'Leave it! Get in the car!'

As he climbed in, Munna saw Kapoor Sahib's

eyes dart up and down the deserted street. He opened the gate, got in the car and backed it out, his jerky movements making the car jump a little. Leaving the gates open behind him, Kapoor Sahib sped off down the road.

'Sir?' ventured Munna hesitantly.

'Hmm.'

'Wouldn't it be better to slow down a little? That way we'll look less suspicious.'

Kapoor Sahib stared at him, then nodded and visibly forced himself to relax. They drove on in silence, more smoothly now. As they turned into the main street, Munna's heart gave a little lift. When things calmed down he would come here and buy the doll ... And then he saw Basha Bhai's toy shop as they drove past it. The sign board sagged grotesquely from one of its hinges, blackened and charred. The shop below it was burned to cinders. Everything. Everything, including Aisha's Doll ...

The next few weeks were tense and frightening. Rafi Bhai's family spent many hours with their ears pressed to the radio listening to the news of the outside world. One Man begged for peace, over and over and over again. The others seemed bent on breaking the country up. Nobody believed that people of different gods could get along together in one land.

It was the month of Ramzan. This year people kept their fast as usual, only now it was easier to control their hunger knowing there was nothing to eat anyway. It had been a while since the people from that area had gone out to work. And even if anyone had the money, there was little out there to buy with it.

The day Basha Bhai's toy shop burned down, Munna had handed over his eight rupees to his father. Rafi had locked it away in the tiny metal safe. Now Munna knew that his father intended to use the money to buy their tickets.

'We are no longer safe here. I know people in Rangoon. They are Abba's old associates and I know they still honour his memory. For his sake they will help me. I'll write to them, and once things are arranged, we'll cross over into Burma and make a new life there,' he had whispered to his wife one night when he thought the children were asleep.

Things were getting more unsafe, and Munna

sensed that it wouldn't be long now before leaving the country became inevitable. On the twenty-seventh roza, the night of Badi Raath, the country officially split in two. Eid was only three days away. If the moon could be sighted, Eid would be on the 18th of August this year. Yet the people rampaged on as the Holy Month drew to its close. The mohallas were burning. People were on fire, within their hearts and without.

On the night of the 17th, somebody mustered up the courage to sneak up to the terrace and peer into the sky. And there he saw it glowing softly, that sliver of a moon in a sky lit up by the fires burning the city. He let out a soft cry that was somewhere between joy and anguish. Then he ran downstairs to tell the others.

Nobody from the mohalla went to the eidgah for the Eid ka namaaz the next morning. It was too unsafe. But they prayed at home, prayed as they had never prayed before. There were no new clothes that year, no sheer khorma. The mohalla was quiet, and greetings were exchanged amongst people of the same building only, for nobody dared venture out into the street.

Ammi and the other women of the building had left-over henna powder from last year. They pooled the powder into one large bowl, mixed it into a thick paste, and sat together in the central courtyard and applied it to each other's hands, talking softly amongst themselves. The men folk leaned over the balconies of each floor to watch, grateful for this momentary happiness their women were enjoying.

Somewhere in the world there are people walking freely in the streets, laughing, talking, thought Munna, as his eyes sought and found his ammi and Ashu among the women. Somewhere out there, maybe in this very city. But not here. Not us.

Then something stirred. There was a subtle shift in the atmosphere. The men began to discuss in sharp whispers, growing more animated with each passing minute. Munna, lost in thought with his chin resting disconsolately on his hand, noticed nothing at first. But as the people around him grew more excited, he raised his head and turned around.

'He's coming!' they were saying.

'Really?'

'*Haan*! He's coming here to beg for peace, to wish us for Eid.'

Munna was curious. So when the others rushed outside, he went along with them.

From a distance, Munna saw a thin old man wearing a dhoti and holding a stick. He had round glasses on his nose, a thin white moustache, and a head with no hair on it. He looked like a man of no importance, yet he was followed by throngs of people, all reaching out to touch him, shake his hands, touch his feet. The old man came closer and closer, and finally he reached the place where Munna was standing. Somebody stepped forward, tears streaming down his face.

'Bapu!' he cried. 'They will wipe us out! We will be destroyed!'

Bapu took the man's hands in both his own. He spoke softly, but with love. 'They are your brothers. They are blinded by hate but they are your brothers. Have faith in God!'

'Bapu,' said another man. 'Are you not afraid to be here alone and unprotected?'

'I am among my own countrymen. Against whom should I seek protection?'

'But you are a . . .'

'I am a child of God,' said Bapu.

'But how to forgive? They have killed our children in this war of hate!' cried one man despairingly.

'Remember one from among them that you have loved in this life. Remember one act of kindness you have received from him, and your wounds will begin to heal.'

Suddenly, Munna's mind jumped to Shankar. It had been weeks since he had thought about him. These days he only thought of people in terms of 'us' and 'them'. But now, with the old man's words, he remembered that little friend he had spent so many hours with in the attic, their shared secrets, the laughter, those innocent eyes. Suddenly he heard Shankar's voice saying, 'Pink sweets! I'd buy a dozen of those pink sweets from Anthony's bakery and all of us at home would eat one.'

Munna turned around and sped inside his building, taking the stairs two at a time. He rushed into his house, dug out the locker keys from its hiding place, unlocked the safe and rummaged about till he found the eight rupees he had given to his father. He withdrew one note and sprinted out of the house again. He ran till he reached the main road. Thanks to Bapu's presence, there was some life in the street. Surely Anthony's bakery would be open? After all, he was a Christian and had nothing to fear.

Ten minutes later, Munna raced back into his mohalla. In his hand was a box of a dozen pink sweets.

His eyes searched for the old man, fearing that he might have left. But he was still there, at the far end of the street, having made his way slowly, stopping to take people by the hand and wish them Eid Mubarak.

Munna hurried up to the old man and said, 'Bapu?'

At the sound of the young voice, Bapu turned.

'Will you be going to Belighata from here?' asked Munna, looking up at the old man.

Bapu nodded. Then Munna held out his hand, offering Bapu the box of sweets.

'Please, will you give this to Shankar? He is my friend. He lives in Saraswati Building. Tell him it is from Munna for Eid.'

Bapu looked down at the box in Munna's hand. For a second he said nothing. But when he took the box and passed a gnarled hand over Munna's tousled head, Munna saw that the old man was crying ...

~

In August 1947, Mahatma Gandhi undertook a fast unto death in Calcutta, to protest against the Hindu-Muslim riots in the city. As he lay in his little bed, weak and dying, a twelve-year-old boy, who was leaving Calcutta for Rangoon with his family, was closely following the reports of Bapu's failing health on the radio.

Bapu, he whispered sadly. Eat something.

One evening, the boy sneaked out of his home and bought a few oranges. Then he made his way through the city, searching for a certain address ... When he found it, he went inside and climbed the narrow flight of stairs that led to the terrace where the Mahatma lay. At the door, the boy stopped and gazed at the thin figure lying motionless in a narrow bed. Then he placed the oranges carefully near the threshold and slipped away.

The next morning, news reached the Mahatma

that people all over the city had stopped rioting so that he would break his fast. When he heard this, the Mahatma smiled weakly. With the last vestiges of strength left in his frail body, he murmured, 'Can I have some orange juice, please?'

Precious Gift

Shahrukh Husain

Tara's teacher, Miss Harman, walked into class.
'Tara,' she said. 'Mrs Delancey would like to see you in her office.'

'Me, Miss Harman?' Tara's mind was like a film on fast-rewind. What had she done?

'Yes, you,' Miss Harman said. 'And get back as quick as you can. Remember you're leading the Eid presentation in class.'

Reluctantly, Tara left the classroom. She flashed a questioning glance at her friend Sita who responded with a little shrug. No help there, then.

Tara had worried all night for her Eid

presentation, now she had something else to worry about. By the time she knocked on Mrs Delancey's door and walked in her mouth was dry. But when she saw her parents sitting there, her stomach did a sickening flip. The Head didn't get parents into the office for nothing. This must be serious.

Mrs Delancey motioned her to a chair and turned to her parents. 'Now that Tara's here, I can explain why I invited you.'

Summoned more like, Tara thought. She glanced quickly at her parents. Dad looked seriously grim—she knew that look, it was rare but usually a bad sign. Mum's expression was, simply, scared. Maybe, Tara thought, she's already told them something.

Mrs Delancey began to speak. 'You know, of course, from Tara's consistently good grades, that she is an exceptionally able pupil,' she said. 'But her talent and skills in French are quite frankly extraordinary.'

Dad looked so relieved, he forgot to smile. Tara cringed as he pulled out a large chequered handkerchief and mopped his brow. Mum was smiling so hard, she'd put a Cheshire cat to shame.

Mrs Delancey continued. 'We have a very special

opportunity this year to send four girls from our school on a gold-star trip to a French resort for this coming Autumn term. Naturally we'd like to offer one of those places to Tara.'

'Thank you, Mrs Delancey!' Tara said, jumping up. Mrs Delancey beamed. 'I thought you'd be pleased. But what do think, Mr and Mrs Hameed?'

'It's a long time on her own away from . . .' Mum said.

'Oh, she'll be well looked after Mrs Hameed. It's a well-run institute. They have a number of tutor-chaperones who will take them out on a daily cultural outing—theatre, film studios, sports training, debates, lectures . . . you name it. The idea is to immerse them pleasurably in all aspects of a well-rounded French lifestyle.'

'But she's only thirteen,' Dad said.

'And so are the other girls who we have chosen.' Tara knew Mrs Delancey's reactions well after two years in secondary school. There it came—the slight furrow of the brow, the finger and thumb at the corner of her mouth a fraction of a second before she spoke. She had moved into patient and patronising mode.

'Believe me, I understand your concerns. We take the safety and well-being of our girls very seriously, too, and let me reassure you, Mr Hameed, the institute in France has many years of experience in these cultural trips.' She pursed her lips, then handed Tara's parents a crisp, pale green envelope. 'Have a look through and let me know what you decide. There's an application form inside if you decide to ... let Tara go. It will be the experience of a lifetime.'

Mrs Delancey stood up and held out her hand. 'Thanks so much for coming,' she said. 'Well done, Tara.'

In class, Miss Harman was talking about the event planned for Eid. It was a very special performance sponsored by the Inter-Faith Centre because the story of the sacrifice occurred in both the *Bible* and the *Koran*. Miss Harman said it was excellent for people to see the similarities in religions as well as the differences.

'Yesssssss!' hissed Tara. 'I've got a place on the French trip!!'

Miss Harman smiled. 'I'm sure the whole class wants to congratulate you, Tara. Well done. Now—

the Eid show. The girls working on the project, please move to the book corner. Pull your chairs round and work on your plans.'

Tara dove into her desk and pulled out the professional looking file her cousin Mehnaz had given her the last time she was in India. When she used it she felt clever, like Mehnaz—Dr Mehnaz.

She opened her file and leaned forward. 'It's lucky my grandmother's here,' she said.

'Bor-ING!' Rena said. 'I want to know about the French trip. Did your parents say yes?'

'You're going skiing, isn't it?' Daisy said. 'You'll meet loads of boys.'

'Boys are rubbish,' Tara said. 'But there are some amazing things on the brochure.'

'There are two Eids,' Tara's voice changed, suddenly, as she spotted Miss Harman coming up to their corner. 'The one that we are working on is at the end of Ramadan and is called Eid-ul-Adha which means the Festival of Sacrifice. It is closely linked to Haj, the most important pilgrimage for Muslims, so Haj has to be an important part of it.' Rena jumped as Miss Harman spoke from behind her. 'Glad to see you working, dears, and not talking about the French trip and boys and skiing.'

Omigod, Tara thought. She *heard* us!

'Okay,' she said. 'This Eid is about sacrifice, to remember that the Prophet Ibrahim (Abraham in the *Bible*) had a dream—or saw a vision—in which he was commanded to sacrifice his son to prove his love for God–Allah. Abraham always obeyed Allah, so he told his son about his dream. Guess what? His son AGREED to be sacrificed. Scary or what?'

'I'd have run,' Sita said. 'Or at least begged him to change his mind.'

'Okay, so look, here's a picture of Mina where Ibrahim was going to sacrifice his son.'

'Do we have to say Abraham in a funny way?' Nicola said. 'Can't we just say Abraham?'

'Muslims say it in Arabic, like it is in the *Koran*,' Tara said. 'Now can I go on please?' She wished Miss Harman would go away. 'So where was I? Oh yeah. On the way there, the Devil—or Shaitan, as we call him—tried to stop Ibrahim from obeying God's command so the Prophet Ibrahim's wife Hajra and his son, threw stones to chase him away.

'Ibrahim laid his son down on a large rock, closed his eyes and struck a blow. Suddenly, a voice said, "You have proved you love Allah above all else." Ibrahim opened his eyes and his son was standing beside him, smiling.'

The group gasped with relief. 'Come on guys. You knew the story already, didn't you? But how scary it would be if we didn't, yeah?'

She handed them some typed papers from her file.

'So the point of Eid-ul-Adha, is to remember Ibrahim's sacrifice. Luckily we don't have to sacrifice kids anymore, but a lot of people in the Muslim world sacrifice sheep or goats and in some Arab countries, they even offer camels.

'Secondly, we need to reflect on the meaning of sacrifice. What does it mean today? That's the bit I find really hard to understand.

'Thirdly, this is a chance to share and give. The sacrificed animal is shared among family and friends—and one third goes to the poor.

'Finally, we should reflect on temptation. When we set out to do something good—or difficult—things get in the way. We should remember what is most important.'

Miss Harman held out her hand for a sheet.

'Good resource,' she said. 'How are you going to present the show?'

Tara looked worried. 'That's the complicated bit. Muslims can't show pictures of the prophets and their families, or act them out.'

'Well, that's a challenge, girls. Work out how you're going to present this as a show. Decide who'll do what and we'll discuss it next week. And here's the good news. You have all term to put your play together.'

During the break, Anna, Ellie and Rekha ran up to Tara. 'We've been selected, too,' they said.

Everyone congratulated the four lucky girls, firing questions. Anna, Rekha and Ellie told them all about it but Tara was silent, wondering what her parents would decide. The four girls got on well and she knew how much fun they would have together.

'You lucky bunnies,' said Sita. 'I'd give anything to go on that trip.' She gave Tara a quick hug. 'You deserve it!'

Tara looked away. 'My parents might not let me go.'

'Why?' asked another girl. 'Cos you lot like to

stick together? Can't be let out without Mummy and Daddy trailing behind.'

Tara whirled around but Sita grabbed her arm. 'Let it go, Tara. She's just jealous.'

'Shut-up, Maureen,' said Ellie. 'You don't know anything. Anyway, my parents probably can't afford to send me.'

'Pauper!' someone yelled. Others took up the refrain. 'Pauper! Pauper!'

'Oh go away and turn green somewhere else,' Ellie yelled back. 'Just because you weren't selected.'

Ellie had dealt well with the nastiness but Tara was troubled. 'Do they all think I can't go because my parents are Indian? Or paupers?' she asked Sita on the way home.

Sita shrugged. 'Do you really care?'

'I never thought I would—but I do. Because it's not true. If Mum and Dad say 'no' it won't be for those reasons.' She clenched her fists. 'But I won't let them say no. I'll make it happen. Mehnaz wouldn't take no for an answer. Do you know, she's moved to a big city now, away from home to work in a grand, new hospital . . .'

'You've told me lots of times,' Sita smiled. 'She's

a shining example to all young Indian women.' She squeezed Tara's arm.

'Well she is,' Tara said, smiling.

~

Dad and Mum were impressed with the institute and its roster of training and activities but not so pleased about the cost.

'How much?' Dad gasped.

'You heard,' Mum said. 'Three thousand pounds.'

'That's ridiculous. For what?'

Tara flicked through the pamphlet. *'For three months your daughter will live the life of a debutante and enjoy all the delights and demands of a young woman of high society.'*

'We're not high society,' Tara's brother Aslam piped up. 'Dad manages a stationery shop and Mum doesn't work anymore. So what you chattin' on about, sis?'

'Shut-up, Aslam.'

'Don't tell your brother to shut up,' Mum and Dad said. They always told her off in chorus.

'Huh! Got you in trouble! So what, you don't

think we good enough for you no more?'

'Stop trying to be cool, Az. You sound like an idiot. Anyway, Mum, Dad. Are we going to do this or not?'

Dad laid his hands flat on the coffee table. 'Sorry my dear. I don't think so.'

Tara left the room without a word. If Mehnaz could convince her parents to let her go to university in the United States, she could convince her parents about a three-month trip to a country across the channel. She would come up with a plan, just like Mehnaz.

~

A few days later, Tara rushed into her living room, excited.

'Mum! Mum! I've got a job helping in the library once a week,' she said. 'And the After-school Club teacher says I can help her get her classroom ready.'

Mum looked surprised, but she was proud, too. She hugged Tara.

'Perseverance pays, so they say. I'll speak to Dad.'

'She'll convince him,' Nani Jan said as Tara helped her dish up the food. 'And it's quite wonderful that you've got yourself these jobs. Young people don't have these opportunities back home. Specially not littl'uns like you.'

She handed her a plate of chapattis for the table. 'Do you know, I've been saving for twelve years to go on Haj? There was always a more urgent use for the money. Now I'm an old woman. I hope I will go next year. If not, then Allah knows I did my best.'

Tara went quiet thinking of the demands she was making on her own parents. Maybe, she thought for the first time ever, they wanted things, too.

After Mum and Dad told Mrs Delancey that Tara would go to France, Tara worked hard at her jobs and kept up her studies. Dad worked longer hours, Mum went back to her old, part-time job at the library and even Aslam offered Tara his pocket money. Meanwhile, Tara and her friends put their minds into producing a good performance for the Eid show. Nani Jan quietly supported them all by taking care of the housework.

The evening before the performance, Tara came

home with Mum and Aslam and found Nani Jan gazing out of the window.

'What's wrong?' Tara asked, throwing her arms around her grandmother.

'Aunty Parveen called.' Nani Jan's voice was dull. 'Mehnaz collapsed at work. Luckily her colleagues are taking good care of her. Aunty Parveen needs to be near her.'

'But the hospital's miles away, Parveen will have to move to the city,' Mum said. 'Who'll take care of the kids and the farm?'

'I will,' Nani Jan said. 'I must book my flight to India as soon as possible.'

Tara felt as if her heart had stopped. Nani Jan's hopes of going to Haj next year were gone. She wanted to cry. Tara couldn't get Mehnaz out of her mind. She had worshipped her cousin since she was a small child. It was Naz who taught her to tell the time, to bake cakes and plant seeds. And if Naz had not helped her with geometry two years ago, she would not be getting top grades in it now.

Tara splashed her face with ice cold water to freshen up after her sleepless night. She was determined not to let her class down. The girls had decided to show how the Prophet Ibrahim and his family were closely linked to different parts of the Haj pilgrimage as well as to Eid-ul-Adha. Tara had based it on Nani Jan's vivid memories and her lively way of storytelling.

The show began with a group of younger children telling the story of the Prophet Ibrahim and his sacrifice. Then it was time for Tara's group.

Proudly, she switched on the PowerPoint, projecting the image of two hills in a rolling desert onto a large screen.

'Look into the distance and you will see in that thick, dark sand-cloud, a trio of tired, bedraggled people. Strain your eyes, to see an elderly man, dragging behind him a great amount of baggage, as he encourages a small boy and a thin woman to continue walking. All around them, stretching for miles and miles, the desert has thrown up golden dunes, like sea waves. "Allah commanded me to bring you and the boy here," says the man. He is the Prophet Ibrahim. The man leads them to a point between two hills and tells his wife he must leave them there.'

"'If it is Allah's will,' says Hajra, 'then He will take care of us,'" continued Tara.

She then stepped back and Sita continued the story. 'After the Prophet Ibrahim left them with food and water, Hajra cared for baby Ismail alone, sheltering him from the sun in the scant shade of the hills. In the end the food ran out, and soon after the water too. Hajra became weak. But she could not bear the ever-fainter cries of her baby, hungry, thirsty, his skin growing hotter by the moment, in the baking desert. Desperately, she ran up and down between the two hillocks of Safa and Marwa looking for water.'

'Then a miracle!' said a chorus of voices.

The screen changed to a close-up shot of a long shadow covering a space at the lower end of a sun-bathed slope.

Sita stepped back and Kelly took up the tale. 'The angel Gabriel was shading the baby from the scorching sun. A tiny bubble of water rose by Ismail's heel and turned into a stream that danced and skipped and sparkled over the parched sand. Ismail was saved. God had seen to it. That spring survives to this day in Makka shareef. It is called Zam-zam.'

As she spoke, a stream bubbled up from the

water on the screen behind her which slowly changed into the modern structure of the Grand Mosque with pilgrims thronging to an enclosed well, holding bottles.

'Centuries later, the stream of Zam-zam still flows,' Nicola explained. 'People say its waters can heal us as they healed baby Ismail.'

The screen image moved over the present, concrete buildings of Safa and Marwa with concrete and ramps and elevators. 'Even today, pilgrims walk between these two hills to mark Hajra's faith.'

Nicola beckoned to her friends. The group bowed. The audience clapped.

'We want to thank Tara's grandmother for telling us all about Haj and the events around it,' said Miss Harman. 'And now Tara has a special thanks to say.'

'Nani Jan, you've taught me about caring and putting others first. It's been hard but I've finally understood what sacrifice is about.'

There was a thunderous clapping and cheering from the audience as the curtain fell.

~

Tara laid her head on Nani Jan's shoulder on the drive home. 'You know when I said I understood about sacrifice at last?' she said.

Nani Jan stroked her hair.

'Well, this is what I've decided. I've saved up a bit of money with that extra job. And Mum and Dad have, too. And we can all afford to go to India with you to look after the kids and Aunty Shirin for the Easter break. And you can still go to Haj next year.'

Nani Jan shook her head. 'That will not be necessary,' she said. 'I booked my ticket today. I would never let you sacrifice your trip.'

'Nani Jan,' Tara said, hugging her grandmother. 'I've been happier than ever before since I made the decision.'

'She'll have lots of opportunities in the future,' Mum said. 'She's just a child, Amma.'

'Funny thing is,' Tara said, 'I feel a lot more grown-up since I had the idea. Sacrifice isn't just about giving up something. I feel like I've got a lot more from it than I'm giving away.'

Red, 17: An Eid Story

Devashish Makhija

Today is Eid.

Which makes the appearance of this coat as rare as an *Eid ka chaand*, thought Nandu to himself. There was a number stitched into the inside of the collar. '17'. That makes the old man—Feroze—one of Rangat's oldest customers.

Nandu let his rough fingers glide gently over the wool. It was an old coat no doubt. There isn't a single readymade shop in the city that sells such a delightful knit anymore. If they do, the coats are branded. And this one isn't. The only identity this coat carries is the '17' cross-stitched intricately with a deep red thread inside the elegant collar. Nandu closed his eyes and let his fingers trail the little loops in the 17. Back in the 70s when this coat must have come in to Rangat for laundering, Liyaqat bhai must have sat down behind this counter when the shop shut, and stitched the customer number in. I would have made a 17 in barely ten pokes of the needle, thought Nandu. But Liyaqat bhai must have taken over ten minutes. And then he would have tugged at each little loop with his needle to check if it was a steadfast stitch. Liyaqat bhai. Tch. For him life lasts forever. So everything he touches should last forever too.

Nandu stepped back, looked at the coat one last time, then started folding it. A cool wind caught the back of his neck from the door and he looked around guiltily to check if anyone had seen him fingering the coat like that. Folded, the dark coat looked handsome. From an angle to the left the coat was jet black. But when seen from a similar angle to the right it magically turned into a deep ink blue. Now Nandu looked wistful. He had tried not to think the thought several times in the last few minutes, but it burst like a balloon filled past its capacity, into his mind now. Feroze was a slight man.

His coat would fit Baiju perfectly.

The crinkly brown paper parcel changed shapes under his arm as he walked. Working at a laundry had its perks. Sifting, folding, unfolding, packing clothes could be strangely therapeutic. Ever since his wife died in the bomb blast three years ago Nandu had been working at 'Rangat'. The blast had spared his life, but had taken his hearing away. This job was the only one that'd have him after he lost his constable's uniform. What use would he be as a protector of the public if he couldn't HEAR the voice of the junta? But the force was kind to him, he still got monthly severance money. And he was free to spend all day at Rangat, quietly tending to other people's second skins ... that came in worse for wear ... and emerged good as new.

He spent the evenings delivering the laundered clothes to their respective owners. It was a responsibility he enjoyed, ensuring that his customers would turn out crisp, clean and creaseless the next morning. But it wasn't a duty he romanticised the way his boss Liyaqat did.

To Liyaqat laundering was a way of permanently cleansing the clothing of the residual auras of the past, so that it would glow with the wearer's aura anew. Along with the business it was this that he inherited from his father, the man who established 'Rangat' in 1938. Nandu sort of liked the foolish self-importance of the old world. The new world attached value to nothing. He had spent over a thousand afternoons behind the Burma teakwood counter in the shop trying to acquaint himself with the people from the clothes they left behind ... thinking of his wife ... the fateful local train ride ... and Baiju.

Afternoons injected him with the courage necessary to face nights.

Baiju will be fifteen next week, thought Nandu as he waited to cross the road near Gowalia Tank. Thanks to the Maharashtra Police he's playing basketball in his break time in a convent school. Or else he'd be squandering his hours over a carom board outside a municipal school. Baiju will be the Commissioner of Police some day. Nandu startled the lady beside him by saying that out loud. He smiled at her helplessly. He could never tell when a thought would escape from his lips without warning. It was a joke his dead ears played on him often.

He stopped at a chai tuppery to ask for directions to the address on the little chit. He held his spectacles in the steam from the boiling tea for a moment and then wiped the lens with his shirt. He blinked hard as he placed the spectacles back on his nose. He had learned to rely on his eyes more and more in the last three years. He had learnt to 'hear' with them. He wondered sometimes how it might be to 'see' with his ears. But he shooed away the thought the minute it crept into his mind.

He remembered Liyaqat noting that Feroze had taken his laundering to some other laundry years ago. The sight of that red 17 had made Liyaqat wistful. All the 'red' customers were either dead or had learnt to rely on washing machines. He had told Nandu that in 1978 when the customer base touched 1000, he had switched to a blue thread. Feroze's coat was the first red he'd seen in a decade. And it seemed like he had never subjected that beautiful coat to a 'top-loaded tumble-dry'. 'And thank god for that,' said Liyaqat, oddly ecstatic.

He was eager to return to the coat its original *'rangat'*. Nandu shook his head indulgently at the memory of that conversation, and though he tried not to, he couldn't help thinking of Baiju again.

And then he turned a corner and froze.

There before him was the building 'Al Husseini' mentioned on the chit. It seemed nearly as old as Rangat. In every window and doorway were clusters of women and children, looking solemn. A strange sight on a festive day, pondered Nandu, as he squeezed his way past a small crowd stuck like flies to the gate ... and saw a corpse, covered in rose petals, on a stretcher about to be hoisted into a corpse van. Nandu seemed to be the only spot of colour floating in a sea of white. He stepped up to the only man there who didn't look grief-struck and inquired 'Bhai, Feroze Aslam?' The man looked at him gravely and nodded. Nandu looked at him for a long awkward moment and then it hit him. He pointed at the janaaza and asked again 'Feroze chacha?' The man looked vacantly up at the first floor and said, 'He was a good man, a very good man.'

Nandu looked at Feroze's dead face ... then at

the brown parcel in his hand ... and then he thought of Baiju. Closing his eyes for a long moment he tried to shut out any thoughts of his son. And when he opened his eyes Feroze had been slid into the van. Now it was leaving the courtyard slowly. Nandu didn't know why but he found himself checking the height and build of each of the men in that courtyard as they filed out solemnly behind the van. They were all either heavy set, broad shouldered or tall. One of the last to exit was a frail middle-aged man, slim, stooped, his eyes unblinking, his hair a shock of white. He seemed like he'd fit into the coat, thought Nandu, as he walked alongside him. 'Were you related to Feroze?' asked Nandu. 'No,' replied the man, pondering each word like he would a morsel, 'I repaired his watches.' Nandu read his lips.

'That's sad,' said Nandu. The man looked alarmed. Nandu pointed at the funeral procession, 'That he's passed, it's sad.'

'I think so,' said the man strangely, and turned and walked away from Nandu and the funeral. Again, Nandu thought of Baiju, stopped by the side, closed his eyes, folded his hands, said a small prayer, wedged the parcel under his arm, turned and left.

'Take the wheat to the chakki, Baiju,' said Nandu, chopping onions and crying copious tears. Slender Baiju turned off the TV immediately, entered the kitchen blinking hard and picked up the sack of wheat, and stopped. 'Why're you crying baba?' he asked, exaggerating his words so his father would read them. Nandu smiled and pointed at the onions. 'But they never made you cry before,' said Baiju.

'They allow you a winter blazer from class 9 no?' asked Nandu. 'Uh—yes, but I'll wear the sweater only, don't worry, I don't feel that cold,' said Baiju hoisting the sack over his shoulder and slipping his feet into his chappals. 'This year you will,' said Baiju, soaking his tears into the shoulder of his shirt. Baiju looked at him strangely. 'It never even gets cold in Mumbai, baba,' he said, and left.

Nandu held up a small cube of the chopped onion, as a fat teardrop hurried down his cheek, free-fell and bathed it clean. Nandu looked at the piece of onion strangely and muttered 'Rangat'.

Nandu unpacked the coat from the brown paper,

unfolded it and hung it on the only wooden hanger in the old steel almirah where he had stored all his wife's sarees and jewellery. He folded the sheet of brown paper, rolled up the thread that had been used to tie the package, and neatly kept them both on the shelf below. Nandu wasted nothing. He believed everything outlasts us. It's us, just us, that don't last forever. The paper would come in handy. So would the thread. For what exactly I'm not sure, thought Nandu, but come in handy it will. In just the same way the coat is going to serve Baiju now that Feroze Aslam has passed. Is that wrong? I don't know. Can a coat 'belong' to a dead man?

That last thought brought Nandu some strength. He liked logic. It filled up the void that emotional turmoil always left behind. It was logic that helped him cope with his wife's death. It was logic that gave him the strength to deal with a world where there was no music. As long as he was alive, he'd have to eat three times a day, sleep six hours at night, bathe, brush his teeth and tend to his son. It was all logical. It had to be done. Heartache and sadness drained him. Logic filled him with hope. And it was logic that said to him in a firm set of words that he could hear—'A. Dead. Man. Does. Not. Need. A. Coat.'

But why then—thought Nandu, as he ate quietly—do I still feel this emptiness? Baiju's eyes were glued to the small colour TV set. On the screen Dhoni was on strike. On top of the TV were Nandu, his wife and six-year-old Baiju sitting on a horse at Juhu chowpatty. Next to the picture was a small trophy, on the base of which was inscribed 'Runners Up—Savio Trophy' and the legend 'Satyamev Jayate'.

'Too much salt,' muttered Nandu at the food, and got up.

The next day was the longest day he'd ever spent inside the cosy confines of Rangat. He sifted the clothes that had come in without lingering over them for too long, he folded the laundered clothes in a hurry, packed them even faster. He didn't want to hear any of the stories that the clothes carried today. He didn't want to guess the kind of people that wore them. He wanted to be distant from them all, from their joys and their losses, their lives, and deaths. He tried, for the first time in three years, to *just* do his job. Liyaqat didn't notice. Liyaqat noticed nothing in the world that was outside of the clothes he tended to. Nandu thought Liyaqat might not even miss him if Nandu were to not come in to work some day. He'd just wait and then hire someone else.

Liyaqat was certainly not going to miss a dead man's coat.

Nandu walked fast that evening. He finished all five deliveries in under an hour. He stopped for a glass of cutting chai. And with the first sip of the ginger-drenched milky tea his mind slowed down. In four days I'll give the coat to Baiju, he told himself, and the smile on his face when he wears it to school, shows it off to his friends ... that smile will warm Feroze's heart wherever he may be now. But that thought brought with it another question—do the dead feel? And if they do, might Feroze miss that coat?

No. Nandu clenched his teeth and downed the rest of the tea in a single gulp. The dead don't feel. The dead don't drink tea. The dead certainly don't miss their coats. Because the dead don't feel the winter chill.

Or the lack of it in Mumbai.

~

Baiju was still fast asleep when Nandu crept out of bed. Nandu hadn't been able to sleep all night with the excitement of the gift. He walked extra slowly, watching the floor, worried that if he knocked something he wouldn't hear it but Baiju would, and he didn't want Baiju to wake up till much later.

Nandu took the coat off the hanger, looked at it lovingly, ran his wiry weather-beaten fingers all over the coat's breast again. He'd lost count of how many times he'd done this in the last one week. And then he carried it to the room where his wife's picture hung on the wall adorned by a sandalwood-flower garland. He held the coat up for her to inspect, and said to her in his mind 'our son's going to look like a commissioner this winter.' He was careful not to move his lips lest he speak too loud. And, anyway, I'm sure Bindu can hear my thoughts, he thought to himself. And then he froze.

The dead don't need coats.

The dead can't hear thoughts.

And the strange emptiness the thought brought pushed a tear out of his eye.

He felt a little dizzy now. He didn't like this. This didn't seem logical. What was he doing with a dead man's coat that didn't belong to him, talking to his dead wife? But then, he thought, just because she's dead doesn't mean she can't feel what I feel? I speak to her every day and it warms my heart. Why's this any different? Can she hear me?

Can a dead man miss his favourite coat?

Nandu walked the fastest he had ever walked in his whole life. It was faster than a trot. In a few minutes he was running. The paper tore in a couple of places exposing the wool of the coat inside. In the slanting light of the dawn sun, the coat shimmered a mysterious dark blue.

He ran through the gates of Al Husseini and quickly grunted up the creaking wooden stairs.

Noor sat in a throne-like cane chair at the large table. The coat lay unfolded on the table before her. She looked at it like a first-time mother would at her just-delivered baby.

Noor was plump. The kind of soft, glowing, taut plump that age cannot ripen with wrinkles. But she was old. The laugh lines on either side of her eyes had evidently gone out of use only recently. She touched the coat lightly, as if expecting it to vanish under her fingers. When it didn't, she pressed her chubby, soft fingers down on it and let them run along the weave. Nandu sat in a chair across from her. He was quiet. A cup before him held tea that had formed a thick brown film on its surface.

And then as he watched, Noor started folding the coat up, said 'thank you', placed it in the brown paper, tied it with the thread, forming an elegant shoelace knot and pushed the parcel towards Nandu.

'I—,' stuttered Nandu.

Noor smiled sadly. 'Feroze had given his favourite camel skin shoes to his old cobbler the previous day. And his gold HMT watch to the only man who refuses to repair a watch unless he gets the original spare parts.'

'I—I don't understand,' stuttered Nandu. Noor apologised and was about to repeat what she had just said with gesticulations this time when Nandu said, 'No, no I followed what you said, but I didn't understand. I . . . I *stole* his coat . . .'

'No,' said Noor, 'he *wanted* you to have it. He

was a pragmatic man. He believed that our things outlive us. So he left his prized possessions in those places where he knew they'd be looked after. He knew he was going to leave for his final holy journey on the day of Eid.'

'H—how do you know?' asked Nandu, slightly bewildered.

'He still speaks to me,' said Noor and smiled again. 'Would you like me to heat up the tea for you?' Nandu just shook his head dumbly, gulped the tea down, picked up the package, said a hurried thank you and ran out the door.

Baiju stood before the large mirror on the wall in Rangat, beaming. Liyaqat watched very curiously as the tailor from the neighbouring shop stretched the measuring tape from Baiju's left shoulder to his right, then turned to the coat—kept open on the counter—and made some marks on it with blue chalk. Baiju turned to Nandu and asked, 'You brought it that day when you were crying, no?'

'What!' said Nandu, taken by surprise.

'I saw you put it in ma's cupboard, but I didn't want to ruin your surprise,' said Baiju shyly. Nandu's eyes moistened over as he grabbed his boy and hugged him tight. 'And it wasn't the onions, no?' asked Baiju laughing.

'You know everything,' said Nandu and playfully pushed him out of the shop, grabbing the school bag off the floor. Behind them the tailor settled onto a stool next to two glasses of chai.

'Nandu,' called out Liyaqat, his brow collecting knits by the second. Baiju stopped Nandu in his tracks, gestured to him that he was being called inside. Nandu poked his head in through the door. Liyaqat took a moment to frame his thoughts, peered at Nandu inquisitively and said, 'This is the red 17.' As if that statement was question enough he said nothing after it, but waited for a reply.

'Yes,' said Nandu, 'an *Eid ka chaand*. Should we change it to blue now?'

About the Authors

Paro Anand has written twenty books for children and she's finally growing up—with her first novel for adults. She runs a programme, Literature in Action, that uses stories in all kinds of exciting ways. Her book, *No Guns at my Son's Funeral*, was on the IBBY Honor List, and *The Little Bird* was selected as one of the *1001 Books to Read Before you Grow Up*. She is also a world record holder for helping children all over the country make the world's longest newspaper.

Siddhartha Sarma is a journalist and writer based in Delhi. His Young Adult novel, *The Grasshopper's Run*, was recently awarded the first ever Vodafone Crossword Children's Award 2009, the shortlist for which had also included his non-fiction work, *103 Journeys, Voyages, Trips and Stuff*.

Samina Mishra is a documentary filmmaker and writer who thinks children's books are serious business. She loves swimming, road trips in the mountains and reading books in the winter sunshine. She is always rushing and wishes that a day had many more hours. She shares a home in New Delhi (ok, Noida!) with Kunal, Imran and Pirate, a handsome neurotic cat.

Lovleen Misra is a writer-actress based in Mumbai. She conducts children's drama and storytelling workshops and has a long career in films, proscenium and street theatre, radio plays and television. Some of her films are *Amu, Loins of Punjab* and *Yuva*. She is remembered for her role as Chhutki in India's first TV soap—*Hum Log*.

Rukhsana Khan was born in Lahore and now lives in Toronto. She is an award-winning author and storyteller with an international reputation. She visits over eighty schools a year and presents to thousands of children from kindergarten to high school. Visit her website at www.rukhsanakhan.com

Adithi Rao returned to India with a degree in Theatre to assist on the Hindi movie, *Satya*. She went on to become a writer/editor on the travel channel of Indya.com. Adithi writes both children's and adult fiction, and for television and films too. Her short stories have been published in various anthologies, and *Shakuntala and Other Stories* was her first book.

Shahrukh Husain has published twenty-one books and fourteen screenplays—but she loves writing for children best of all. She often visits schools to tell stories or talk about her books—and never publishes a children's book without getting the opinion of a group of children. She spent her childhood in India and Pakistan and now lives in London.

Devashish Makhija is bewildered by the world, curious about little things (like why is the 'butter-fly' not referred to as the 'flutter-by'), and makes films, does graphic-art, stands on his head each morning, and sings to the Bombay pigeons every night. His alter ego resides at www.nakedindianfakir.com